Layout and graphics by Nicoletta Azzolini
Some of the design are by Freepik (artwork by renata.s, lyolya_profitrolya, starline, Designerhrenov, saragnzalez and Terdpongvector)

ISBN-13: 978-0-692-98855-8

Jeanette Nyberg

Draw your own

DAMN

COLORING BOOK

ArtMakesPeople.com

INTRODUCTION

Coloring books are cool.

These are the reasons I love seeing them:

- People are choosing to spend time offline.

- People are making things with their hands.

- Coloring and doodling helps you retain and understand information you might be hearing.

- Pens and markers and colored pencils are awesome.

- Coloring can be the gateway to making other art.

- Coloring is relaxing and everyone can benefit from that.

- Artists who make coloring books are able to make money from selling their art to other people.

- Anything that gets this popular that encourages creativity is exciting.

I've been mulling over for a while if I should add a coloring book to the already saturated market. I did make a few coloring pages that I made available for free, but I got the feeling that I wanted to do something more. Something a level above providing coloring sheets, but not so complicated that people would be scared to try it.

The idea came screaming to me one day: THE PEOPLE SHOULD DRAW THEIR OWN COLORING BOOKS! (Yes, I am fond of the capslock button.)

This idea still makes me excited, even after finishing the book. I am so proud of this book I could spit, and I am giddy like a rabid squirrel to see what people draw (and color) from it. I want to see kid drawings, adult drawings, even your pet elephant can join in the fun.

The idea behind this book is to give you the ideas - the framework - for how to draw really cool coloring pages, and break it down so it's so easy you want to start immediately. As you immerse yourself in the drawing process, you will see how many directions you can take each project in. You can make hundreds of different coloring pages starting with the same basic directions!

I propose that even if you don't consider yourself gifted in art, you can still follow my easy directions. You will find that drawing can be fun and totally, mind-bendingly relaxing to soothe your frazzled nerves. Plus, then you get to color in what you've drawn. We've got the zen supercombo of tangling and coloring right here in one book. You will probably pass out from all the relaxation.

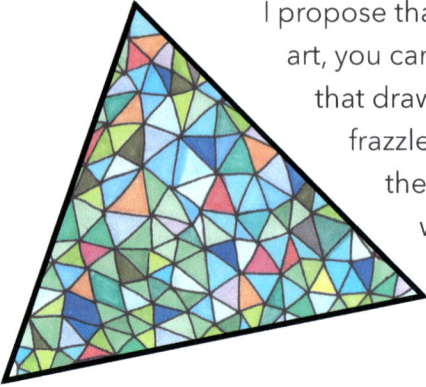

Tips for getting more
out of each project

- You can keep your drawings simple, or add in more lines and shapes to give yourself intricate coloring pages.

- You can scan and print copies of your drawings as you go so you can experiment with adding different lines or shapes, without worrying that you're ruining anything.

- PRINT YOUR FAVORITE DRAWING 3 TIMES AND TRY DIFFERENT COLOR SCHEMES ON EACH PRINT-OUT.

- If you feel moved to deviate from the directions and take your drawings in a totally new direction, go for it. My directions are just there to give you, well, direction, and I'm wondering how many times I can write direction in one sentence.

- In fact, challenge yourself to start some of the drawings as I've described, then see how you can change them to make them completely different than my examples.

These are like DRAWING PUZZLES.
That's so cool.

WHY draw AND color ?

Something amazing happens when you can turn your brain off and just draw for a while. The active meditative state you'll find yourself in feels great. This goes beyond simple coloring - which is relaxing- I think something about making the drawings you are coloring in taps into another part of your creative brain that gives you so much more satisfaction.

All of these drawings, despite how intricate they might look at first, are simple as pie to draw. Just follow each step, and you'll be able to draw all of them. Some take a little longer than others, but relax into the process. You can also scan and print as many copies of your finished drawings as you'd like - give them away as presents, make cards, frame them.

A fun idea would be to have a drawing club, which is much cooler than a book club, especially for people who can't read. Meet monthly at someone's house or an awesome bar and draw and color your little hearts out. I also require that you send me photos of your groups, because I want to live vicariously through your fun. :)

Mistakes will happen.

Sometimes after drawing 20 leaves, you'll draw a really dumb-looking leaf, or your pen will get away from you as you try to finish up that pattern.

This is okay and fine and good. This is also why you didn't just go out and buy a pre-made coloring book.

Drawing is part of the process here, and imperfections happen in drawing.

You have a few options here:

- Scream a long string of incomprehensible curse words while simultaneously crumpling your paper, turning over your table, and shooting red hot fire out of your eyeballs.

- Shrug and leave your mistake in there because who the heck really cares.

- Start over.

- Look at your mistake and take your drawing in a new direction.

- Stare at your mistake while speed-blinking and hyperventilating.

I THINK THESE ARE ALL WINNERS, SO PICK YOUR OPTION AND ENJOY!

MATERIALS:

 1. Sharpies or Micron pens (both are waterproof when dry)
....

 2. White card stock
....

 3. Ruler - I used a stainless steel ruler throughout this book, - it's 1 1/4" wide
....

 4. Pencil
....

 5. Eraser
....

 6. Items around your house to trace: bowls, cups, Duran Duran CD
....

 7. Your choice of coloring-in tools: colored pencils, markers, water-colors, watercolor crayons, pastel pencils, crayons, gel pens, carefully ground herbs and spices
....

PROJECT 1

Let's ease into this whole drawing thing with what is probably the ultimate in simple coloring designs, and is SO FUN to draw.

1.   Draw dots across your page.
I freehanded all mine.
Just kidding.

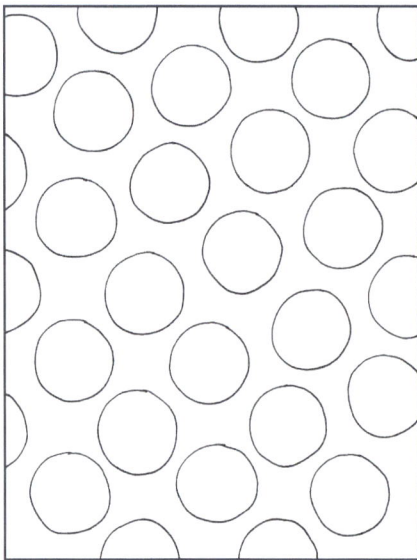

2.   Draw inside the dots.
All sorts of neato drawings.

SING WHILE
YOU DRAW.

SWITCH
IT UP:

Try to come up with a fresh new design for each circle innard. OR! Connect your circles with a background design.

PROJECT 2

Next up is a straightforward, yet titillating exploration of straight lines.

1.   Using your ruler, separate your page into an 'x' with lines going from corner to corner.

2.   Draw lines going down the center from top to bottom and left to right.

3.   Keep your ruler parallel to the diagonal lines, and draw ruler-width lines out to the corners.

4.   Repeat this going the other way (starting with the other diagonal line).

5.   Now do the same thing, ruler-width by ruler-width, out from each of the straight middle lines. Now you'll have some sort of fancy plaid.

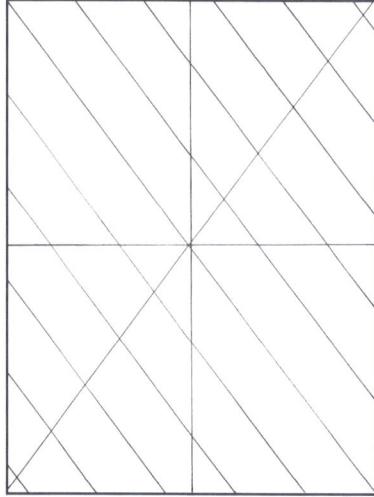

SWITCH IT UP:

Doodle inside the empty spaces, either randomly or symmetrically balanced.

Draw lines halfway between all the existing lines for a tighter plaid.

Trace around some random object in the center of your page for an unexpected break from the even pattern. (Try your hand!)

12

Project 3

You have an excuse here to go buy some new magazines, so don't pass that up, folks.

1.   Grab a magazine photo of a face, or print one out yourself.

2.   Take a piece of your white card stock, and lay it over the top of your photo, against a window or lightbox.

3.   Trace the simple outlines of the face, including the nose and mouth and eyes. Don't bother with all the details in the hair, etc.

4.   After you've traced, take the paper and look at where you can segment it. You'll want to break it up into smaller shapes that will be interesting to color in.

SWITCH IT UP:

If you'd like, try one with straight lines, and one with more curvy lines and see which looks more fun to color in. I used a ruler to make the lines super-straight and severe.

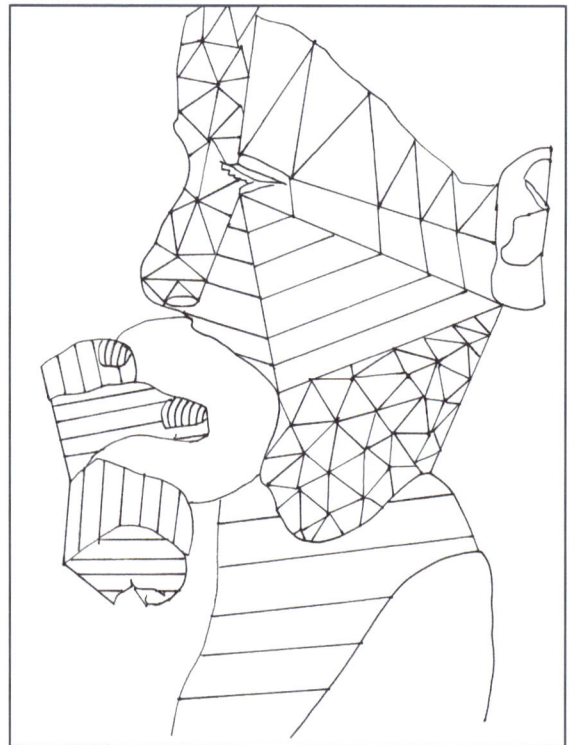

Project 4

When you look at this finished drawing, think of all the directions you can go in with your colors to make this amazing!

1. Break your paper up into an even grid with pencil lines. I used my ruler, eyeballed where the center was, and drew ruler-width stripes out from there.

2. Draw a diamond in every other square, in a checkerboard pattern, and ink each one. Ink the squares in alternating columns as shown.

3. In the remaining squares, draw snowflakes! Connect each corner and diamond point to diamond point.

4. Erase your lines - isn't it pretty?

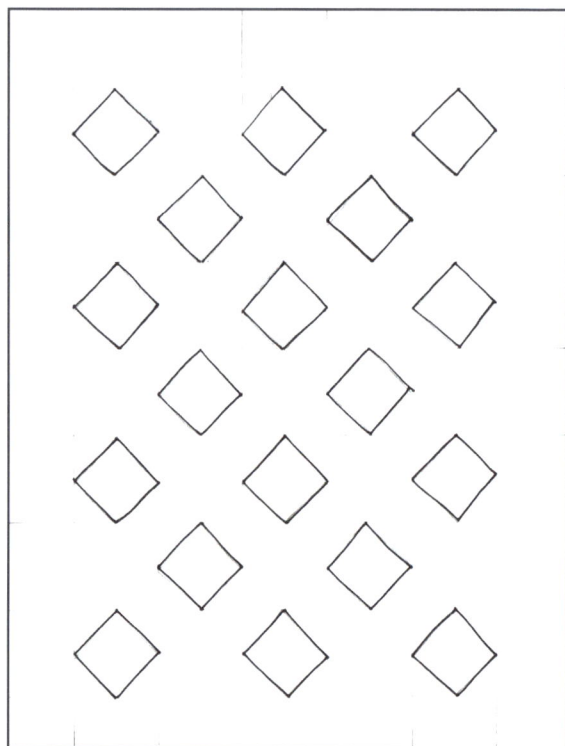

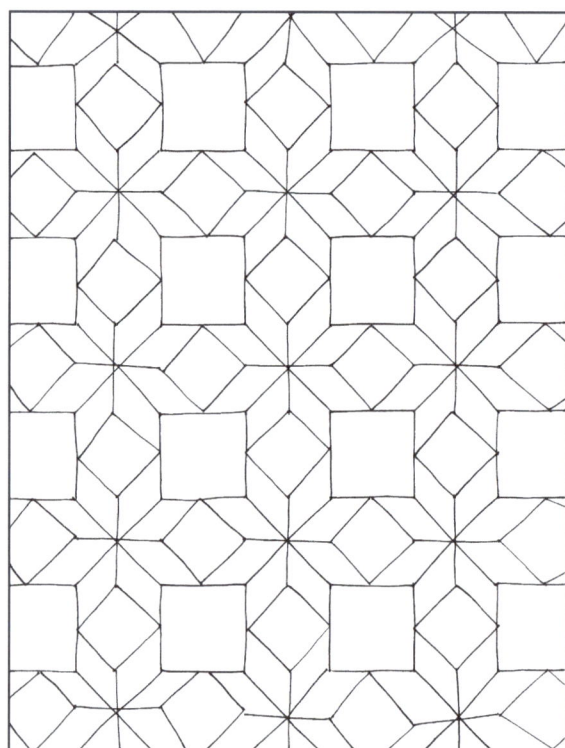

SWITCH IT UP:

You have plenty of ways to switch it up with this one by varying your color schemes, eh?

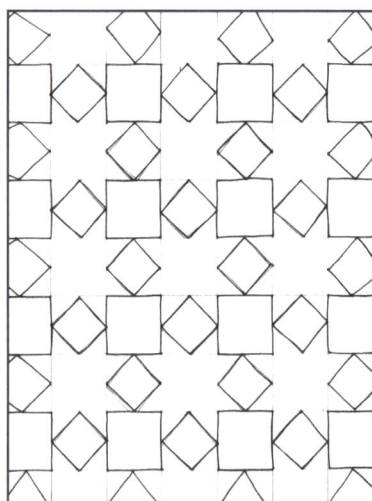

PROJECT 5

Eyes! We are making giant, fantastic, abstract eye designs to color in.

1.   Trace around a salad plate three times. Start with a circle at the top, then do one at the bottom, then a middle one so you can center it on the first two.

2.   Trace a mug in the center bottom with pencil, then trace an 'eyelid' over about ¼ of the eyeball with a dinner plate.

3.   Time to doodle! I drew many eye shapes, which alternated looking like lemons and eyes as I drew them. I also drew triangles to mimic the look of eyelashes. Ooooh abstraction!

4.   Finally, I filled in the eyeball area with lines.

SWITCH IT UP:

This would be a great opportunity to make all the smaller eyes look like actual eyes instead of just suggestions of eyes, don't you think?

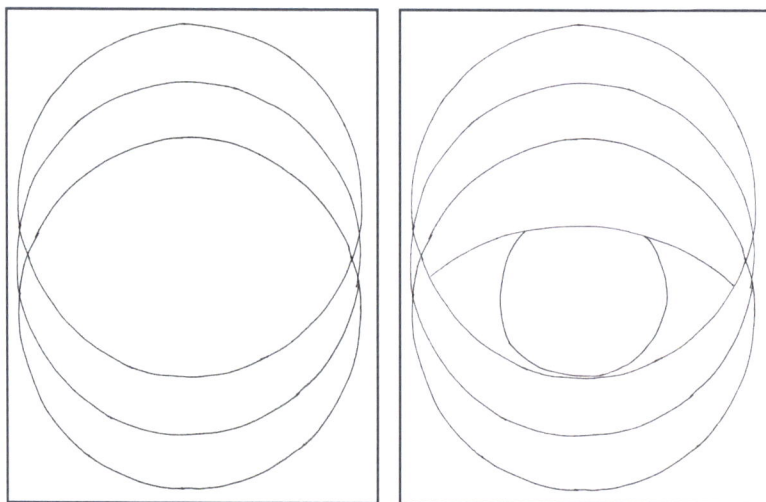

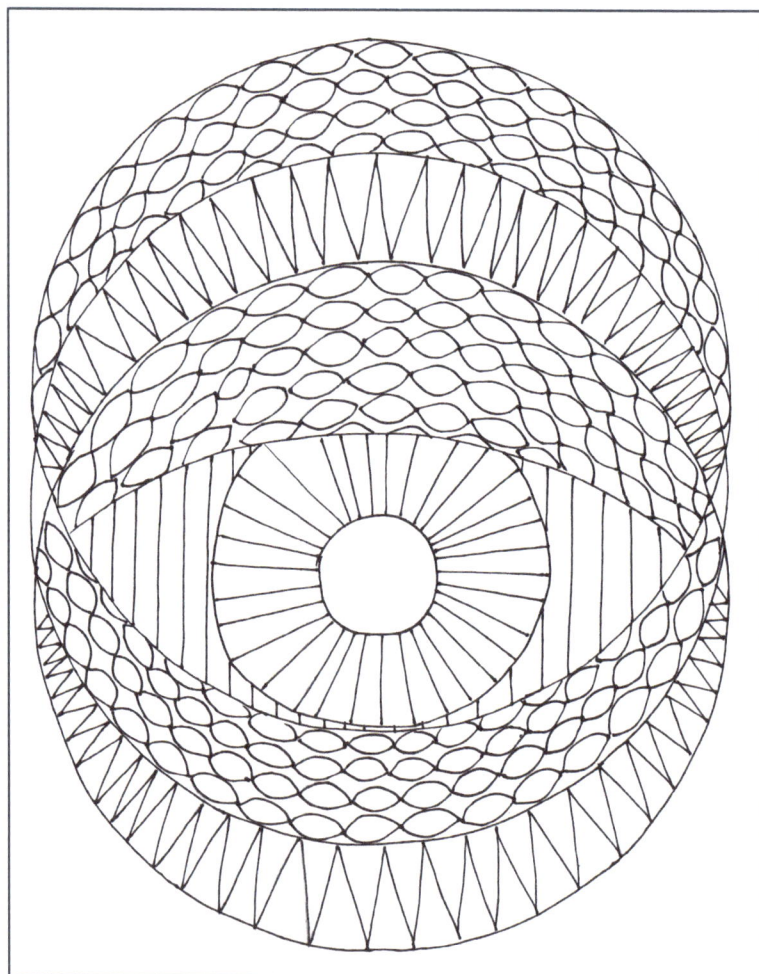

Project 6

This drawing involves lines all over the page. Unlike any of the other projects in this book. LOL, boy.

1. Using your pencil, draw lines all over the page. Make them start on one edge of the paper and go off another edge.

2. Double up each line by drawing another line right next to it, so your lines will look like overlapping ribbons.

3. Go through and erase some lines where the ribbons intersect. This will make it look like they are going over and under each other.

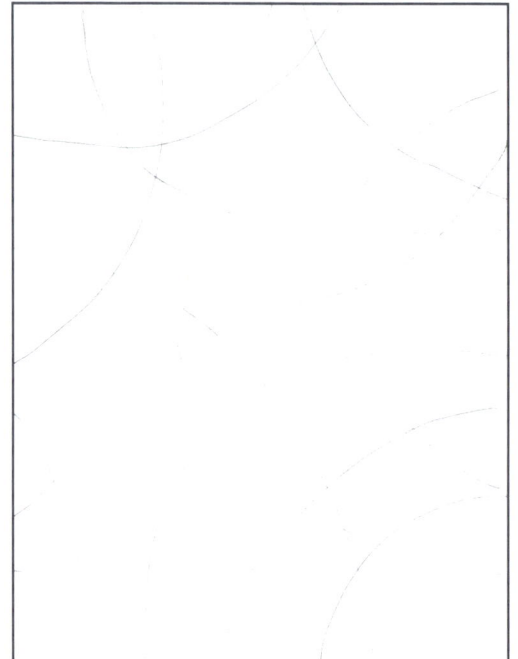

4. I went in with my pencil after this and added a few more u-shaped ribbons on the edges of the paper.

5. Ink it!

SWITCH IT UP:

Doodle in little shapes on some or all of the lines, or in between the lines, or make the lines straight instead of curved.

Project 7

This one is adapted from my Kids Drawing Book, Tangle Art and Drawing Games for Kids.
Why? Because it's cool, it's fun to draw, and it's fun to color.

1.   Draw an 'X' in the center of your paper

2.   Next, start to draw some smaller lines coming out from the 'x'.

3.   Keep drawing connecting lines all over the page.

4.   Take a nap.

5.   Phew, this has been a hard day. Begin to close up most of the shapes with more lines, either straight or curved to get different effects.

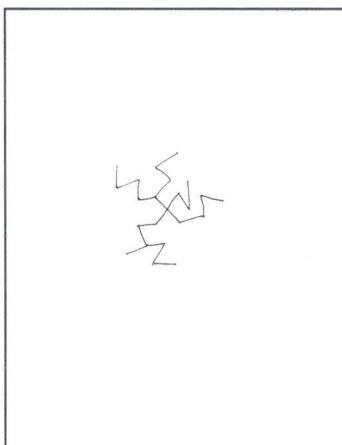

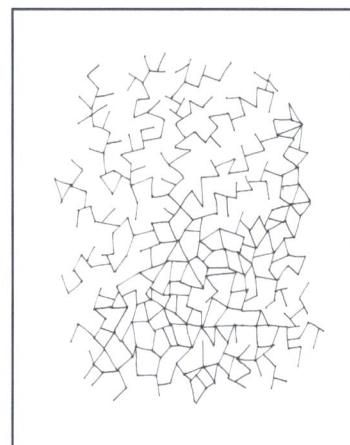

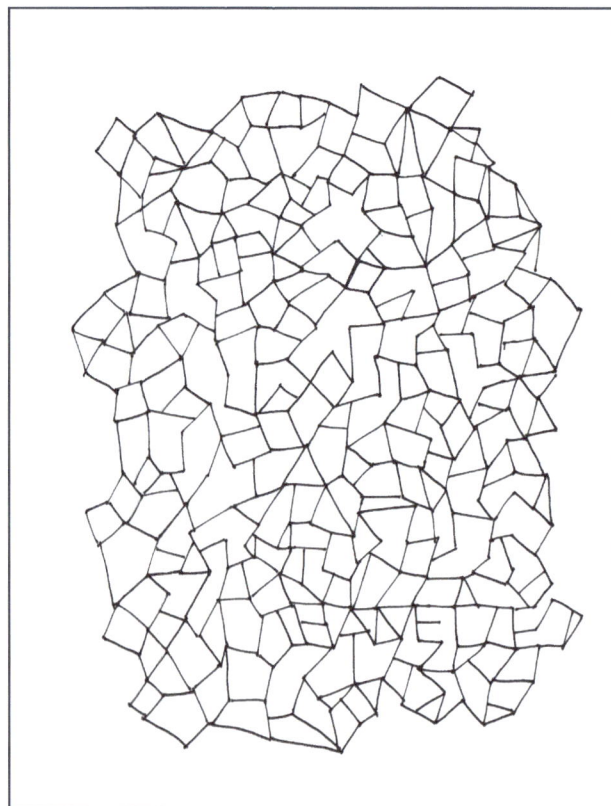

TOP SECRET ELEMENT:

Write your name in there somewhere, hidden in and amongst all the lines. Not that I did. Oh yes, I did. Hee.

Project 8

I like this drawing, because you get to play with the space that is made when circles intersect. Always a good time.

1. Trace around a mug or similar size, in the formation of a six pack. Mmmmmm

2. Trace 2 more times over the diamond shapes that you created in step one.

3. Vary the directions of your lines to emphasize the different spaces.

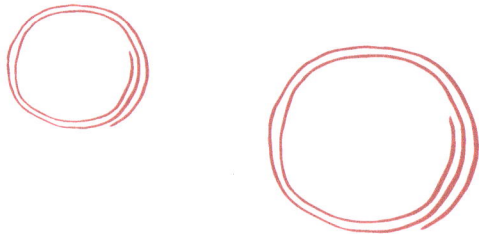

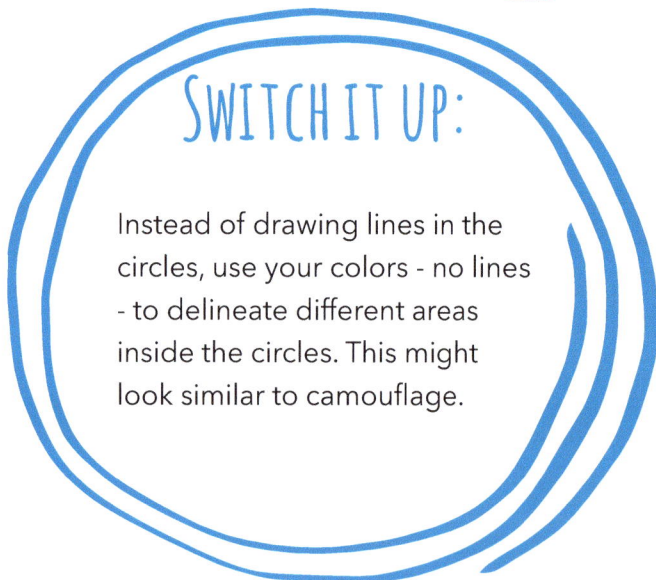

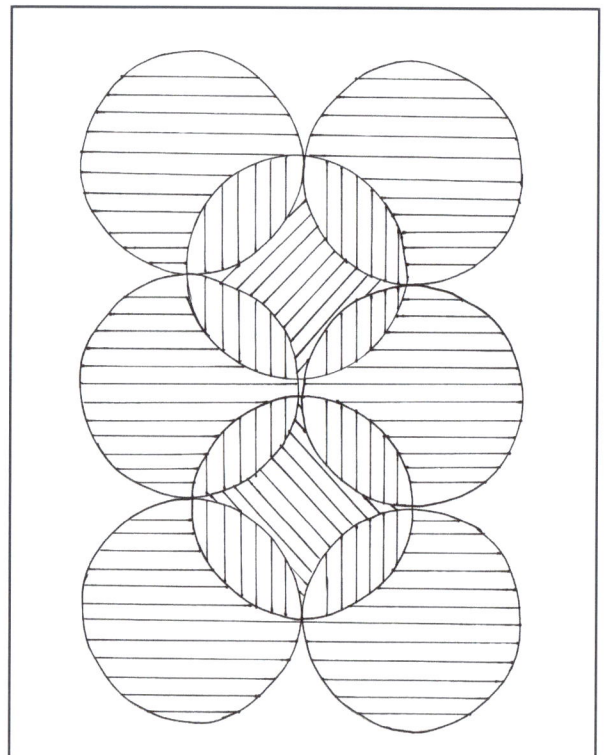

Switch it up:

Instead of drawing lines in the circles, use your colors - no lines - to delineate different areas inside the circles. This might look similar to camouflage.

24

PROJECT 9

You get to make a quasi-mandala drawing here, and fall in love with drawing shapes out from a central starting point to make a mesmerizing design.

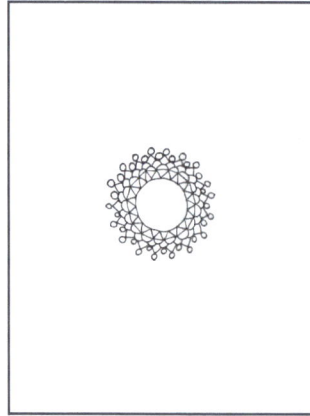

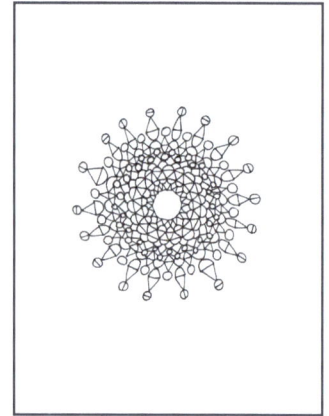

1. Start by drawing a small circle in the center of your page. I traced around a strange blue bottle of dog toothpaste, and not very successfully. It was one of those tracings where your hand slips and you end up shooting lines out all over the place. #amateurhour

2. Anyhoodle, we're going to get ad lib here. Meaning: You probably won't want to follow all of my shapes that I draw exactly. You'll probably want to go into your own doodling zen zone. Start drawing shapes out from the center.

3. If you do want to follow my shapes exactly, have at it, but that sounds stressful.

4. If you want me to just get you started, here: Draw triangles all around the center circle. Next, draw lines to close up the triangles and make more triangles. Next, draw little half-circles around those.

5. Oh yeah, I also drew some shapes inside the circle, so it wasn't a giant, empty circle.

6. The thing about drawing out from a central circle, is that it looks cool at every step of the way.

7. I got pretty intricate with this one, because sometimes you're in the mood to color intricate designs.

SWITCH IT UP:

Limit yourself to 2 or 3 shapes to use in your drawing; try different variations of this using different shape groups. Or try making the whole design only using circles of different sizes.

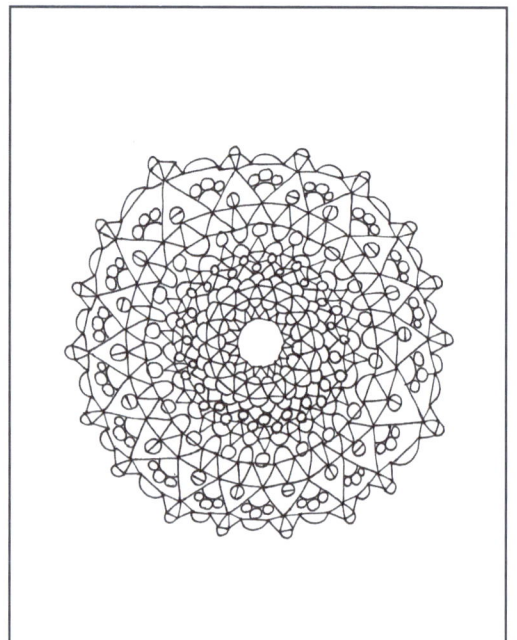

Project 10

Instructions

I took the same starting point as with the last project, but decided to go simpler, so you can see that you can start at the same point with so many of these drawings, and take them in a zillion different directions.

1. Draw the center circle.

2. Stick to using only triangles, circles, and half-circles, but now draw them in layers. For example: semi-circles for a few rows, triangles for a few rows, etc.

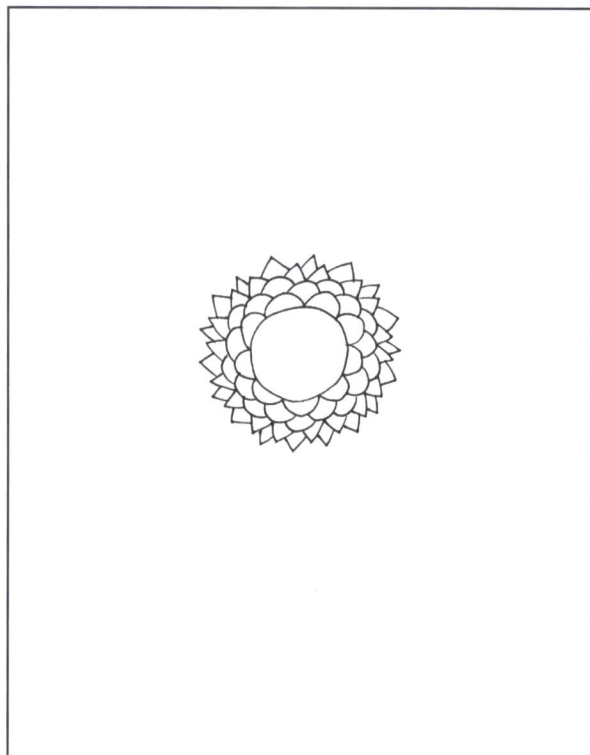

Switch it up:

No extra switch it up here. This IS the switch it up.

Project 11

Let's get nicely geometric and make tile shapes.
GRAB A RULER!

1. Draw a border on your page using the width of the ruler on each edge of the page.

2. Separate inside the border into boxes with your ruler. I started horizontally - draw a line evenly separating the top line and bottom line. Draw another line halfway between those lines, etc, then do the same thing with your vertical lines. That's how mathy I get.

3. Next, draw little half-circles on each inside line in each box. I made mine with pencil first, then drew over them with ink. You get into a little rhythm after drawing a few and you can choose whether you like them to be fuller or flatter half-circles.

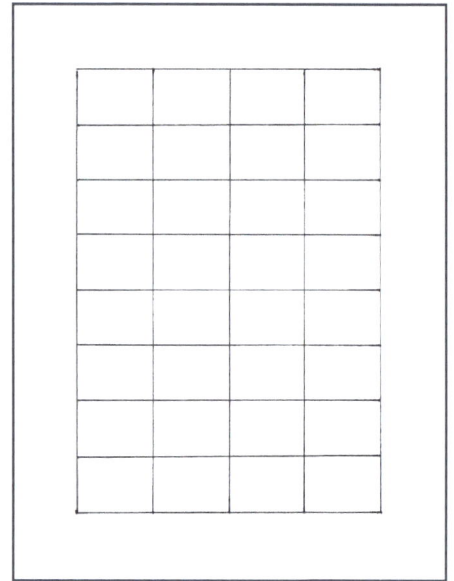

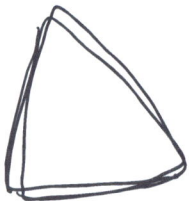

SWITCH IT UP:

Change up the design by adding circles into the centers of the rectangles, or drawing more half-circles inside the existing half-circles.

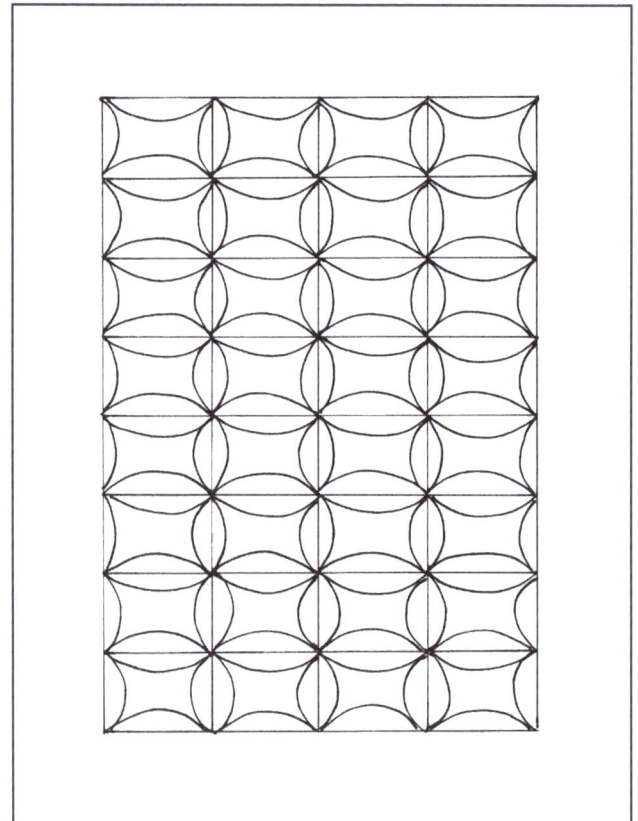

Project 12

Have you drawn a leaf before? I feel like most people probably have. They are easy to draw, and with a little bit of variation, you can fill a page with them in no time!

1.   Start with a couple of leaves in the center of your page. Leaves are basically teardrop shapes, so you can start there and add some lines for the veins.

2.   Add leaves, playing around with how they are situated on the page, and what their shapes are.

3.   And who ever said that leaves have to all have all straight-line veins? How about some pattern!?!

TIPS:

Repeat some leaf designs for more consistency, or draw as many different leaves as you can think up. Draw them in pencil first, and then go over them all in marker. Start with the large leaves first, then fill in blank areas with smaller leaves.

32

Project 13

This coloring page is inspired by a work by Ningura Napurrula, an Aboriginal artist. We will focus on the beauty of the shapes without diving into the meaning of them. (Unless you want to look her up!)

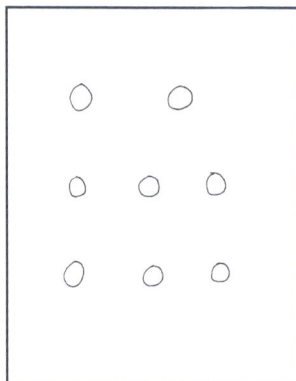

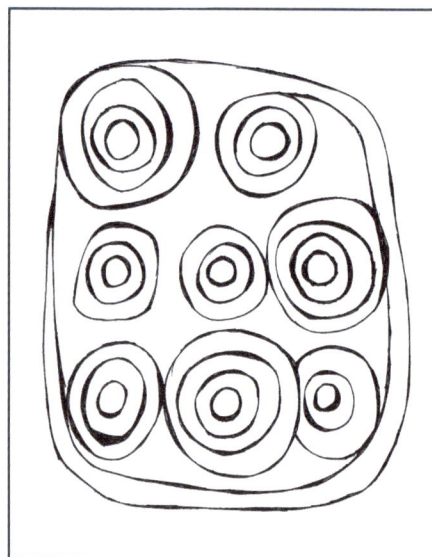

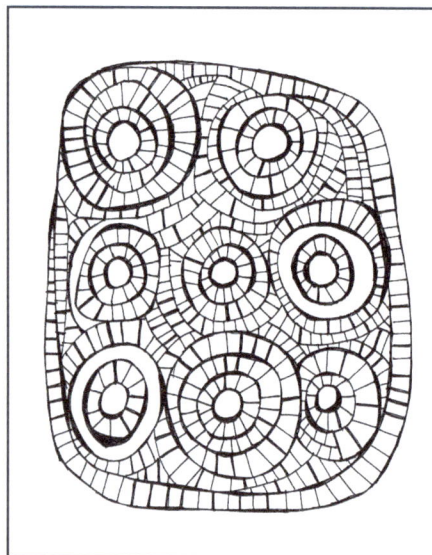

Start by drawing 8-9 circles spread out across your page.

Okay, ready?!

This is where it gets all patterny and fun. Draw out from those circles with concentric circles.

Don't try to make your shapes perfect. You want them irregular and loose. Dancing all over the page.
Vary the thickness of the lines in some areas to add interest.
I used an Ultra Fine Sharpie to give the thicker areas of the lines some cool scratchy texture.

Now you can add some lines flowing around your circles, and draw lines inside some of your paths. I went back in and darkened up some of the small lines, but you don't need to. It looks great without that, too.

I just couldn't stop drawing...

Switch it up:

Draw shapes instead of lines inside the concentric lines and paths.

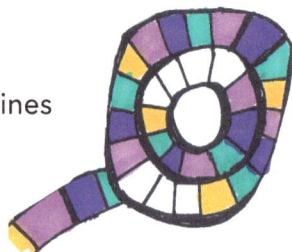

Project 14

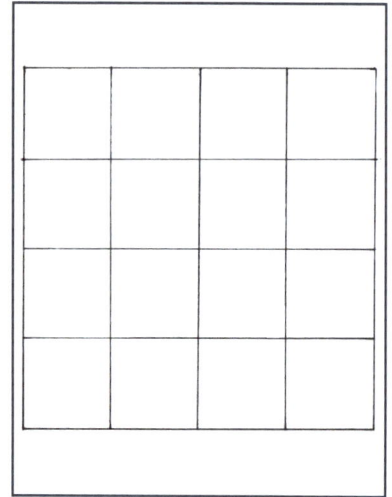

You can probably tell by now that I REALLY like geometric patterns. I hope you do, too, because here is a coloring page idea based on a tile pattern.

1. Draw an 8" x 8" square in the center of your paper. I measured 1 ½" in from each short edge, and ¼" from each long edge of the paper, drew with pencil, and went over it with my ink.

2. Separate the big square into 16 small squares, which is easy because each square is 2" x 2".

3. Now separate each of these 16 squares into 4 smaller squares (mark your pencil lines every inch across the grid), but just draw the lines in pencil, no ink.

4. Draw half-circles in a pattern as shown. I used pencil first, so I could even them out a bit, but now is the time to remember you are not a robot. You are a human, and your semicircles will not be perfect. And that is okay because we are hand-drawing these and it is FUN.

5. Go over the lines in ink, and now is your time to make a big decision: erase your pencil lines or go over them with ink, depending on the look you want. I erased mine. I'm not gonna say that's how I roll, but it is.

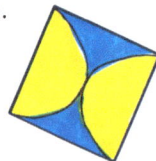

Switch it up:

Vary the directions your semicircles are going, and see what sorts of cool patterns you can come up with, then design a line of ceramic tiles for your bathroom floor.

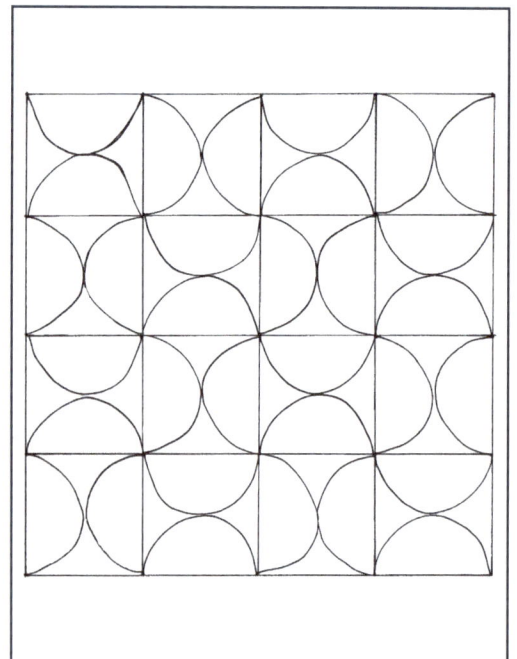

PROJECT 15

Do you remember how fun it is to draw 3-d boxes? I remember the feeling of my little mind being blown when I first learned how to draw one. Then I couldn't stop drawing them, and my elementary school years went by in a blur of cube-drawing.

1. Draw a cube.

2. Draw more cubes connected to that first cube, and fill up your paper.

3. This gets weird and confusing if you try to make too much of a regular pattern out of it - or maybe that's just me. Anyway, I drew random cubes together wherever I could make them fit, and didn't worry if they didn't line up perfectly. I like that looseness about this coloring page.

4. Remember how to draw a cube? Draw 2 squares as shown, then connect the corners with 4 lines.

SWITCH IT UP:

Make long chains of cubes by adding a new square to the last square you drew, and connect them. Does that make sense? Probably not.

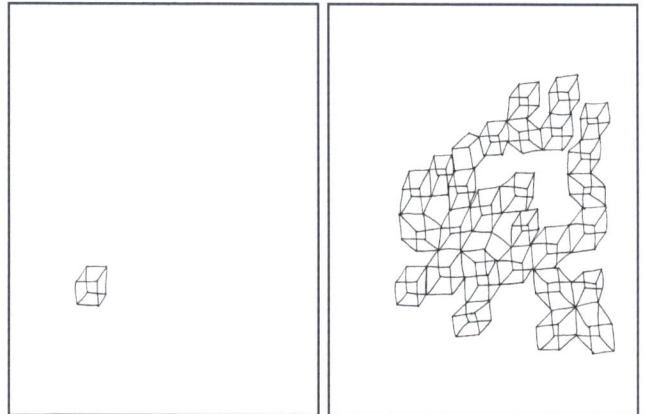

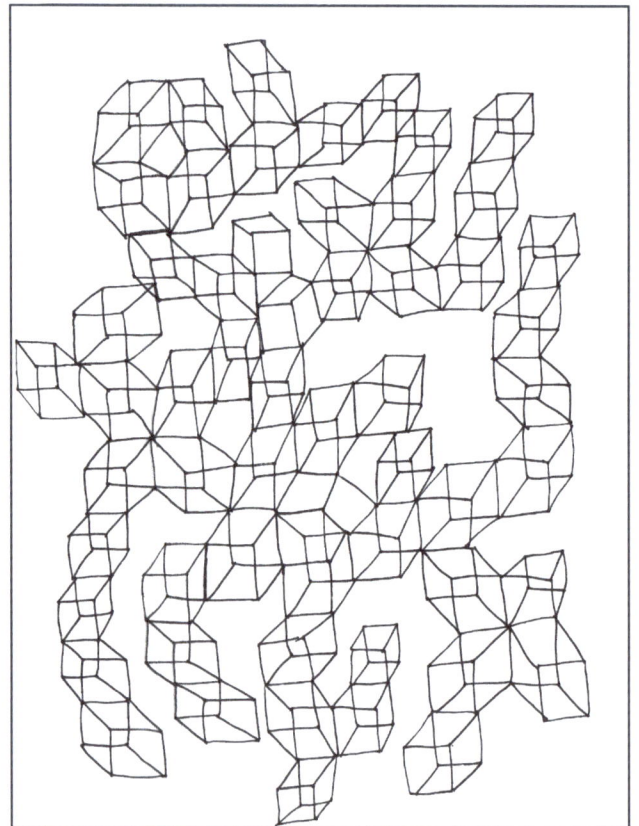

PROJECT 16

I love when drawing pages look obsessive and over-the-top, as with this riot of leaves.

1. Begin by drawing two leaves.

2. Add a few more leaves with stems.

3. Keep a-going.

4. Most of these have stems going back to the middle, giving a really cool dark central area.

5. Turn the paper around as you draw, to evenly draw leaves out from the center.

6. Stop when you feel deep in your heart that the time is right to stop.

SWITCH IT UP:

Draw your leaves all swirling in a gentle spiral around the page.

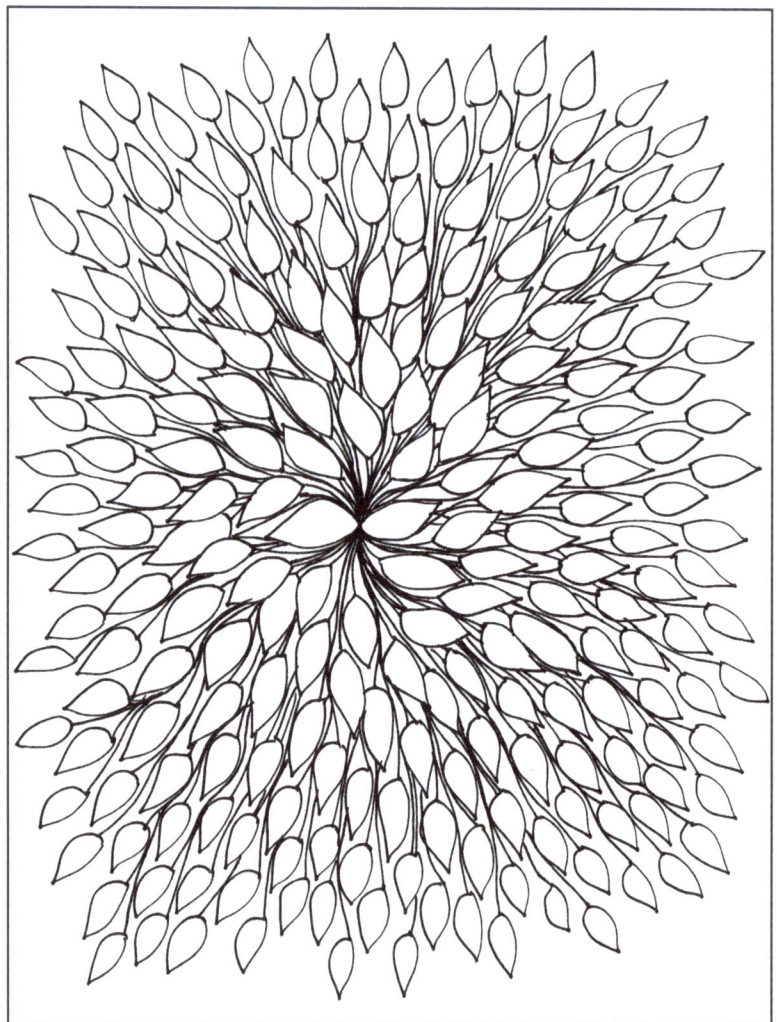

Project 17

Kitchen objects are probably my favorite tools to use to get a coloring page started quickly.

1. Draw around a salad plate

2. Draw around a mug where the outside is touching the outside line of the bigger circle.

3. You may want to stop here and turn this into a face. A big, creepy, bug-eyed face. Or:

4. Draw around the mug two more times, overlapping the first two mug circles, and spread out around the first circle. Get a load of that symmetry. Makes me salivate. And yes, I used a pencil first, because my hand goes all sorts of shaky when I try to trace around round objects. P.S. Rubbing alcohol takes ink marks off of plates and mugs.

5. One more mug traced in the center.

6. Four more mugs creating four 'corners'. It looks good if you want to stop here and color, but I had a problem stopping, so I added:

7. Two more mugs top and bottom.

8. Four more mugs in the corners, thereby taking this design completely excessive.

9. See how it's off-center? This is what's fun about drawing your own coloring pages - this is meditative, easy drawing, it's not perfectly computerized, and you get to discover and play with lines and patterns.

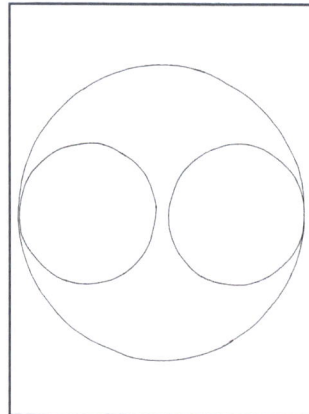

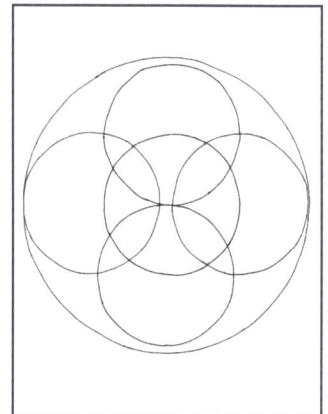

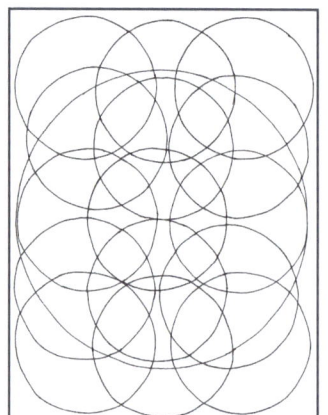

SWITCH IT UP:

See how many circles you can make in your pattern before it looks too crowded like Target on a Saturday afternoon.

Project 18

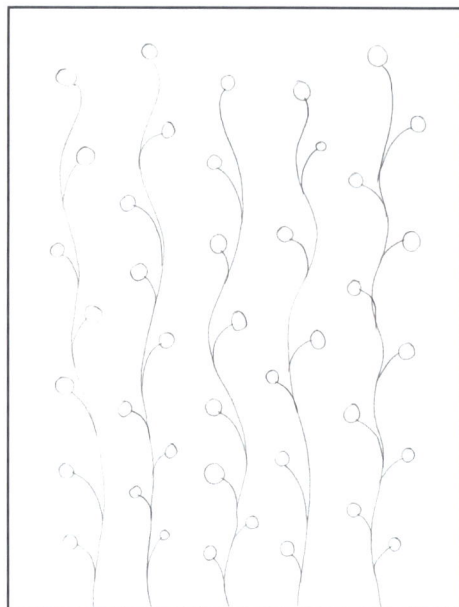

We're going to grow a vertical flower garden now.

1. Start at the bottom of your page, and pencil-draw some stems with circles on the ends. Keep adding more stems with circles as you go on up the page. Doesn't it feel good to have such a green thumb?

2. Now get all doodly-tangly and ink the circles and the petals on your flowers.

3. Go back and ink all your stems now, inking behind any flower petals that intersect the stems.

4. You can choose your style with these flowers. I made this one whimsical, but you can make one flowy and beautiful if you like.

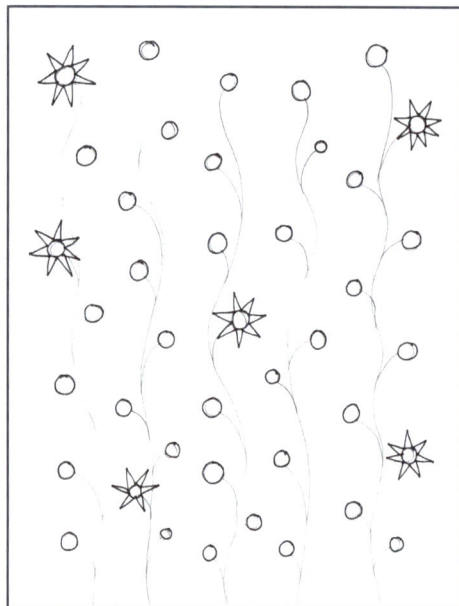

Switch it up:

Challenge yourself to make each flower different from the rest, make them all the same, or something in between. Here's a little composition tip: if you decide to make some look the same, draw those first, and spread them out evenly over the page before you go on to the next style.

Project 19

This is so cool! It took me forever to figure out how to draw these cubes on the page, but when I did it was the most satisfying feeling ever.

1. Separate your paper into vertical pencil lines a ruler's width apart. I eyeballed where the center of the page was, and drew out from there.

2. Add diagonal pencil ruler lines at about the steepness/angle shown.

3. Draw horizontal chains of diamonds with your ink as shown. The bottom little diamond on his own is just to show you where I drew diamonds in relation to the pencil lines. You are drawing over some pencil lines and over some empty space, connecting corners.

4. Ink over all the little vertical lines that do not cross through a diamond. Erase your pencil and do a little jig, because this is cool looking!

SWITCH IT UP:

Color the cubes in 3 different shades of the same color, or add a bunch more lines to make it all Op Art looking.

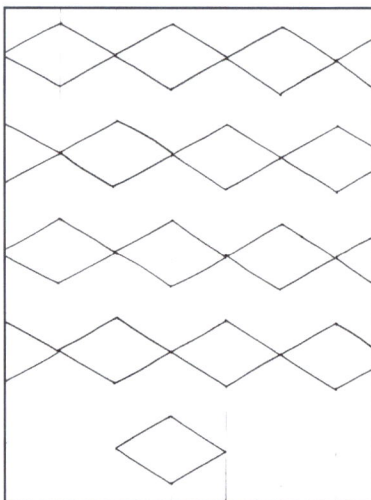

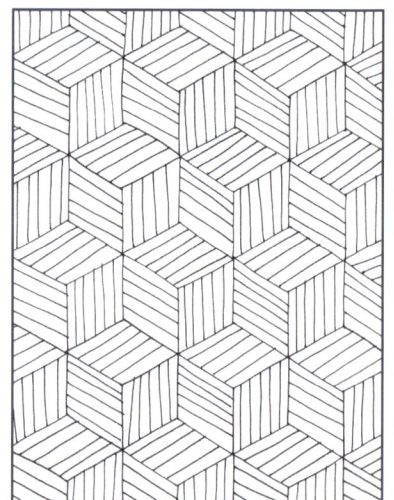

46

47

PROJECT 20

When you look at this finished drawing, think of all the directions you can go in with your colors to make this amazing!

1.   Grid your paper with your ruler and pencil, starting with your ruler lines in the center and moving outward to the edges. (This centers your grid so you won't be left with a bigger space on one side.)

2.   Freehand draw circles (Or trace something small like a penny) on the center of each line intersection. I feel like there's a better word for that. Where the lines cross? Whatev.

3.   Let's now make flowers. On every other circle, draw an inner circle. On the remaining circles, draw circles around your penny circles.

4.   Throw on a podcast and draw many little lines inside the circles.

5.   Draw petals around the little circles, and more circles inside the large circles.

6.   Now the big circles need petals, and you have flowers everywhere.

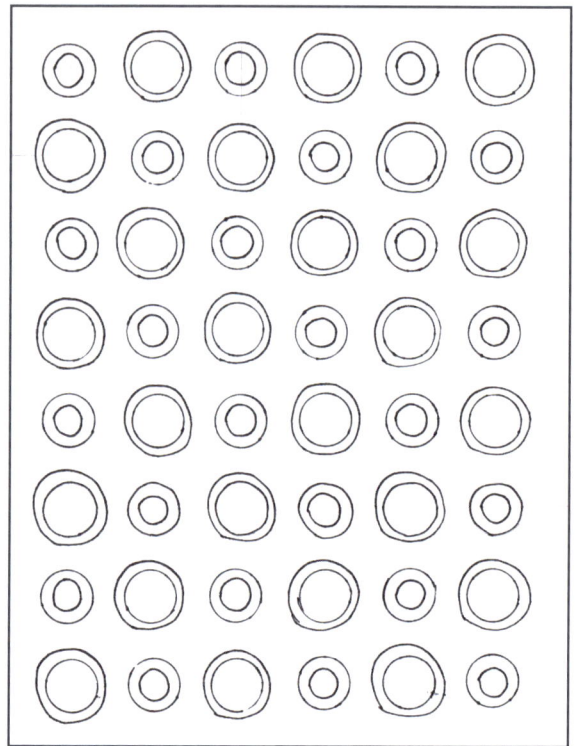

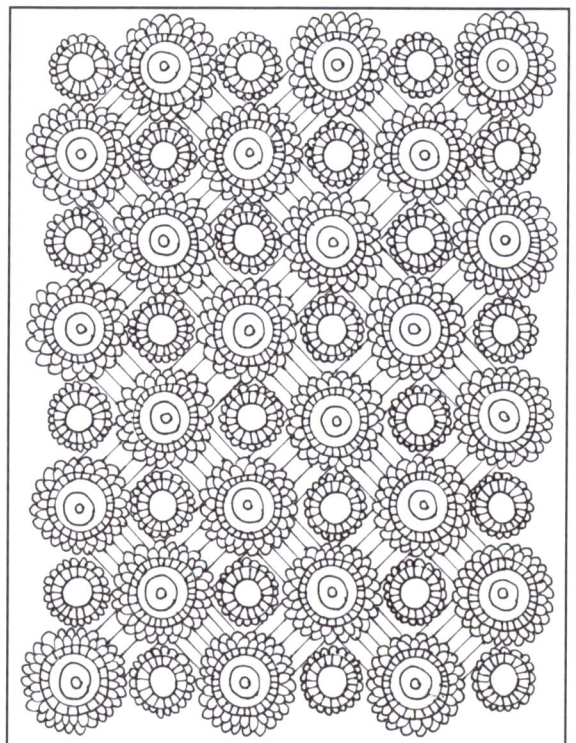

SWITCH IT UP:

Add in some lines connecting the flowers together for more little spaces to color.

48

Project 21

This is where amoebae meet flowers meet peppermint candy. It's all very organic, and loosey goosey.

1.   Lightly pencil draw a bunch of fried-egg looking shapes on your page. You can cover your entire page, or leave a border as I did. Start by laying out a few large eggs, then fill in the empty areas with medium and small eggs.

2.   Erase some of the lines where overlapping happens, so some look like they are in the foreground, and others in the background.

3.   Ink the lines, then go in and draw pinwheel lines coming out from the centers of your blobs.

4.   Now go ahead and say out loud what sort of sound these would make if they were living creatures. That's right. They're your friends.

SWITCH IT UP:

Make different shapes in the centers of your eggs instead of circles, or keep some of them unlined.

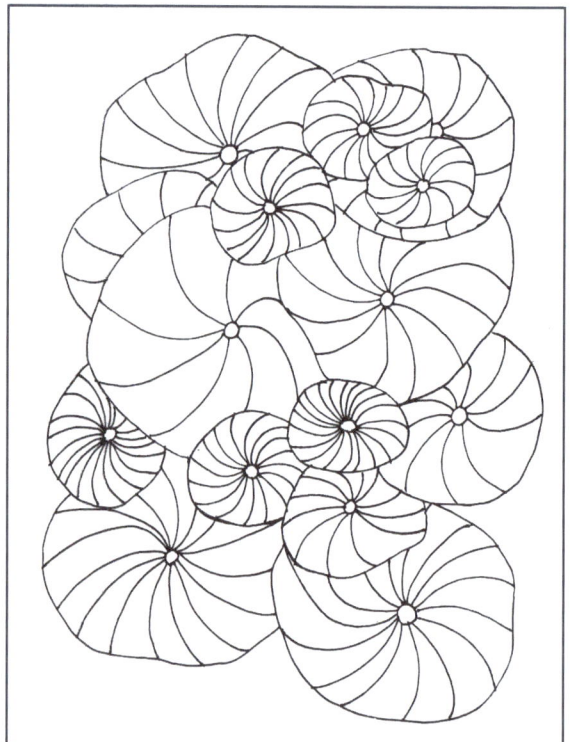

51

PROJECT 22

This drawing has you focusing not only on the pattern you are drawing, but the negative space created in between the flowers. A.R.T.Y. You ain't got no alibi! You're arty!

1.   Grid your page vertically and horizontally with a pencil and ruler. Just use the width of the ruler so you don't have to measure, because measuring is hard and hurts the brain.

2.   Draw little tiny circles on the center of each grid line, as shown.

3.   Color them in.

4.   Just kidding! There's more to this project.

5.   Draw little flowers around each circle. I drew the flowers you see because I like how they fit together and create cool negative space. It makes a great pattern. But you can draw any shape flowers you want.

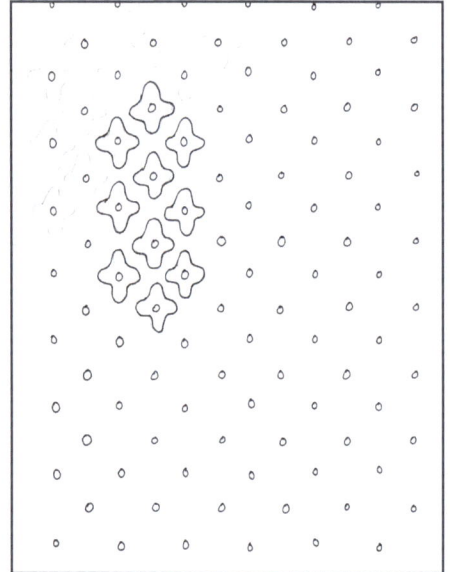

TIP:

I drew all my flowers in pencil first, then outlined them with ink and erased the pencil. You obviously can just jump in and use ink to begin with, but for some reason this flower shape tended to get away from me if I wasn't careful.

SWITCH IT UP:

Play around with different sizes of your flowers to vary the look of the pattern (and the negative space).

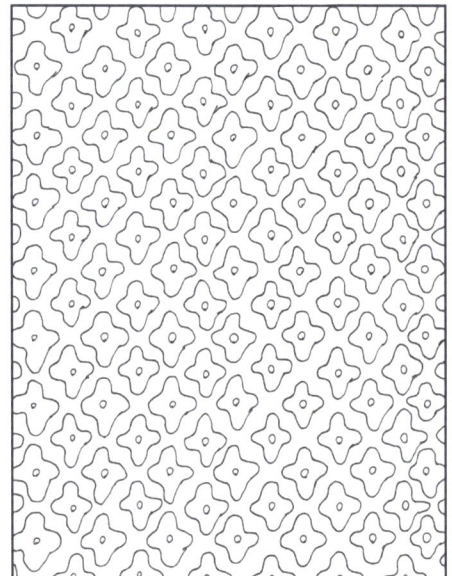

Project 23

I'm going to call this something of a reverse mandala design. You work inward from a large outside circle instead of working outward from a center point. Ooooooh rebelling feels good.

1. Trace around a circle of some sort with pencil. Since I am in a hotel room, I used the lid to the ice bucket, but go ahead and use a plate or something else nearby.

2. Use your ink to draw inside the circle, moving inward with each layer of drawings.

3. Don't forget to erase your outer circle.

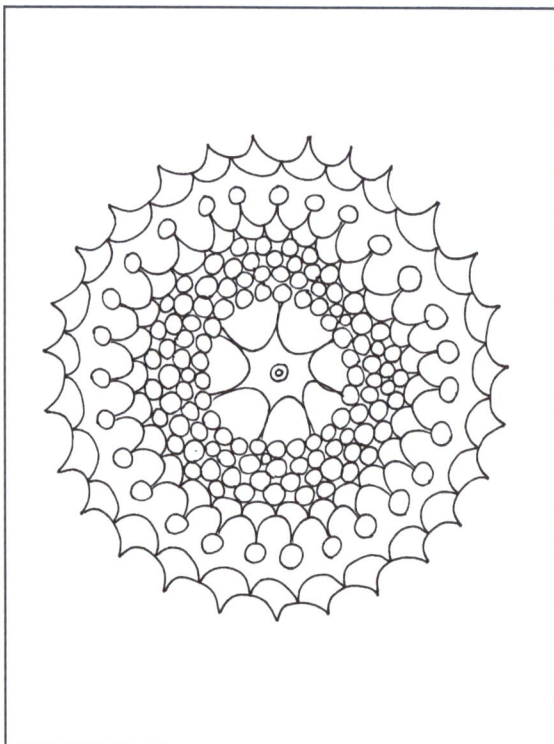

SWITCH IT UP:

Make your outer shapes more dramatic to emphasize where the outer circle line once was.

PROJECT 24

Think 'quilt' when you draw this page. It's a never ending sea of triangles, just waiting for your drawings and colorings.

1. Draw a steep diagonal pencil-grid all over your page, then draw horizontal lines to make triangles.

2. Now ink over your triangles. You can use the ruler to ink over all the lines at once, but I prefer to draw over each triangle line freehand, as it looks a little more loose. I'm weird, though, so do whatever.

3. Focus on every other triangle to fill in with doodles. Keep the other triangles minimal with drawing, and you'll end up with a lovely pattern.

4. Now go buy your fabric and sew up a giant quilt.

SWITCH IT UP:

Fill in ALL the triangles with patterns; try to get the patterns to continue through the triangles in a coherent way.

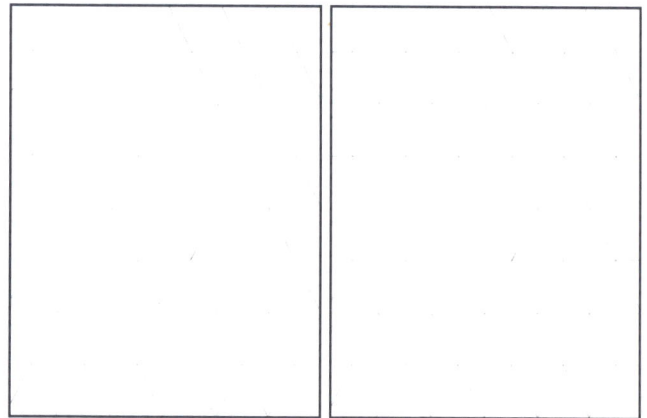

Project 25

Let's draw fish! This is similar to the leaf page, in that we are drawing a page full of objects. But these will be lovely little fish, and they will want you to color them.

Draw fish on your page. The end.

P.S. It occurred to me that fish bodies can have similar shapes to leaves, so if you already drew the leaf page, you should be a pro at drawing this shape.

P.P.S. Fish can be tricky. I did a lot of erasing while I was drawing. It helped to not worry about if I was drawing fish that looked real, and instead focused on whether or not I liked the shape I was drawing.

Switch it up:

Draw chairs instead of fish. Ha.

58

Project 26

We're about to get all trippy with a bunch of meandering lines.

1. Draw a few tiny blobby shapes in the center area of your paper.

2. Draw concentric lines going out from each one. Watch them grow!

3. Add new shapes as you grow weary of drawing lines around your existing shapes.

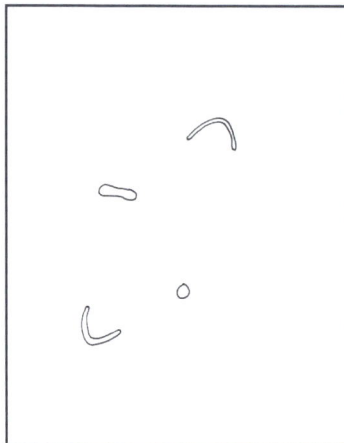

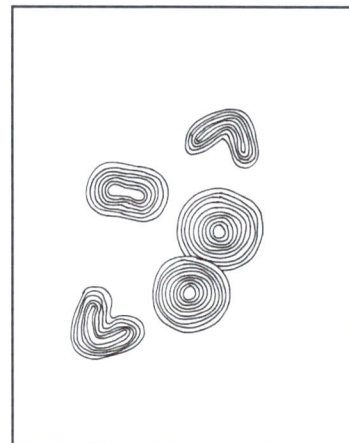

Switch it up:

Start with one blob in the center of your page, and draw out from just that one shape.

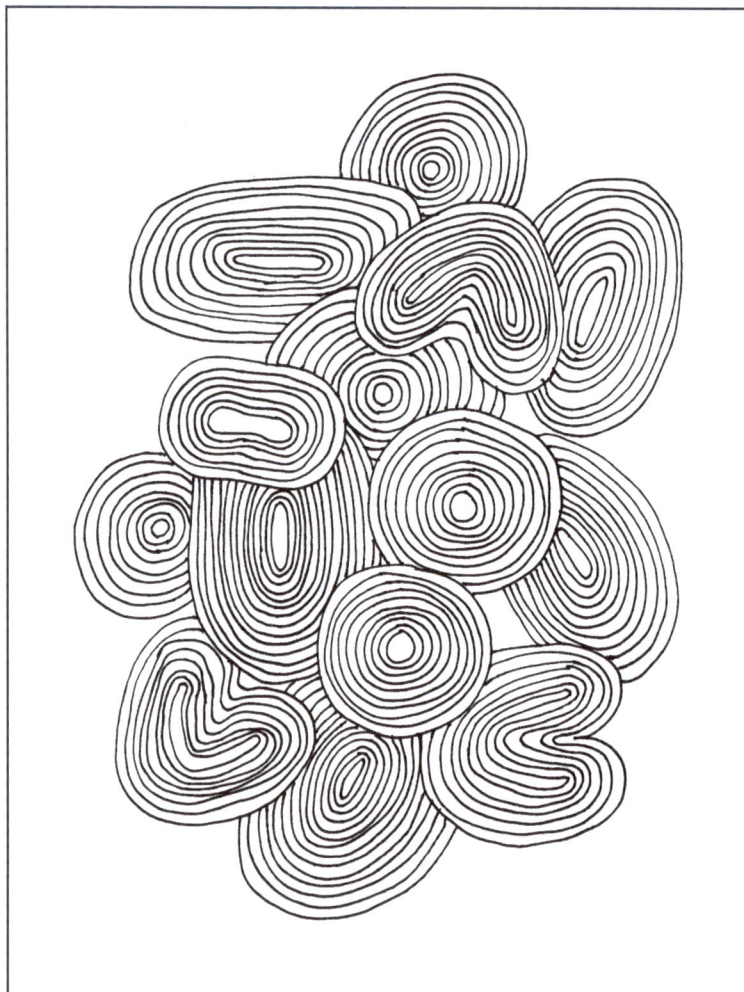

60

Project 27

Instructions

This is some sort of wonky mandala. Maybe not really a mandala- more of a wonky target. I felt the need to shift the design off-center a little and keep it going out forever and ever. Or at least for a little bit.

1.   Draw a little circle somewhere not in the center of the page.

2.   Add more circles around it, but not evenly. I traced around a variety of round objects.

3.   Draw around it and outward, following the circle shape, using all sorts of wonderful designs and doodles. You can look up mandala designs and emulate those, or go more modern/graphic like I did.

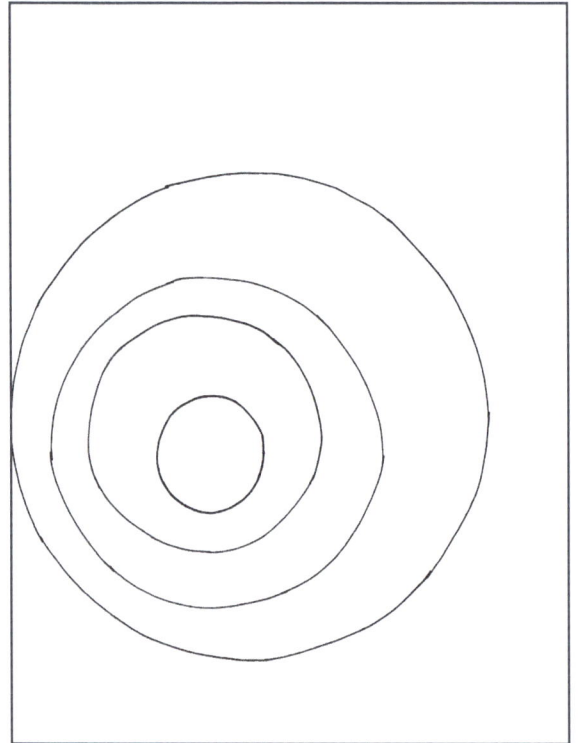

SWITCH IT UP:

Write words inside the circles, trying to make them look as abstract as you can.

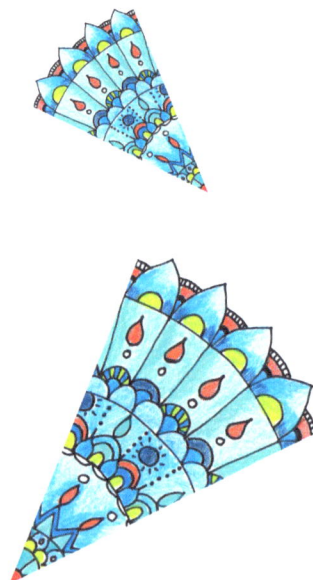

Project 28

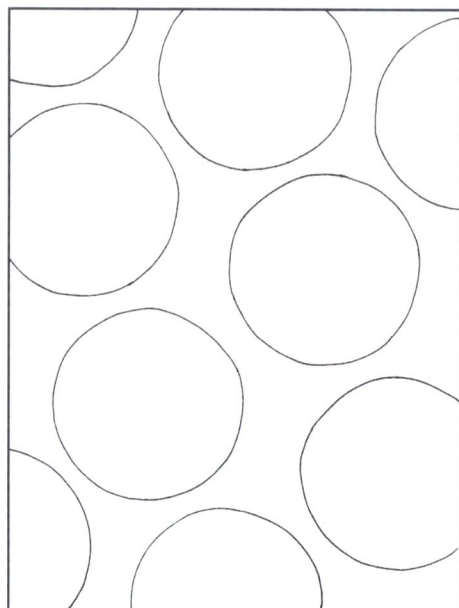

More! Dots! Dots! Are! Fun!

1. Make a polka dot pattern on your paper by tracing around a cup or something around that size. And yes, every time I trace around something, I have to use pencil first or I end up making a mistake.

2. Trace background circles around something smaller. Might I suggest a small round pencil sharpener with attached waste container?

3. Now use your ruler to draw ruler-width lines vertically, horizontally, and both ways diagonally, but only draw inside the large circles.

4. Have fun coloring this riot of lines.

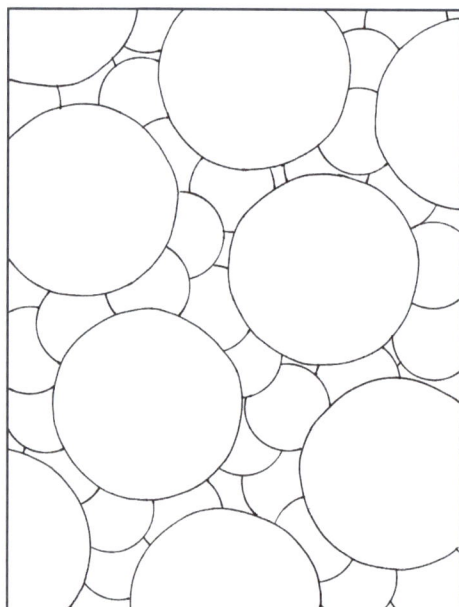

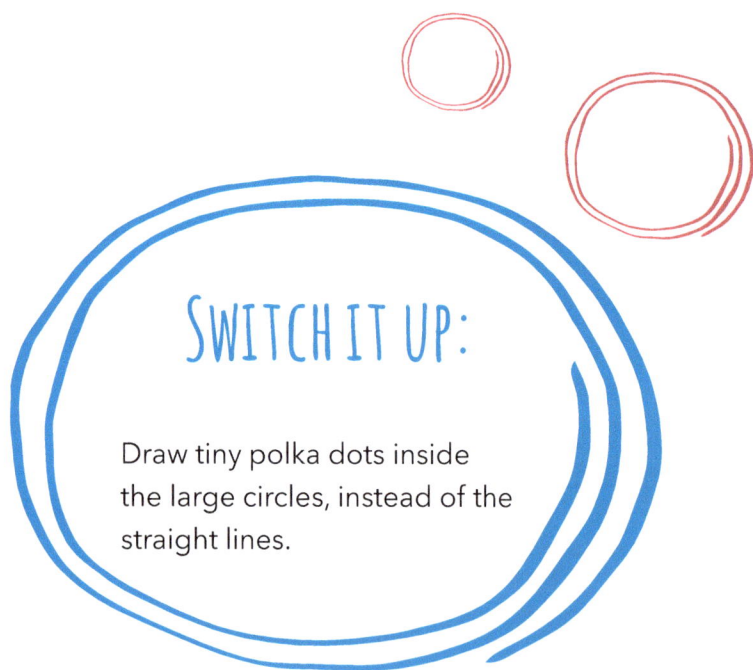

Switch it up:

Draw tiny polka dots inside the large circles, instead of the straight lines.

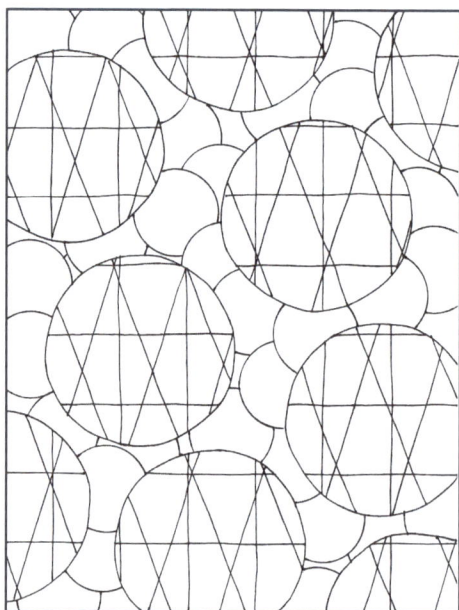

65

Project 29

Cute little flowers everywhere are always good to draw. These are actually so fun and so simple, and I bet you'll continue drawing them everywhere after you've done this page.

1.   Make a frame around your page, or skip it. I wanted something to contain all that cuteness.

2.   Draw out some tiny circles and draw petals around each one. You'll get into a cool rhythm of petal drawing by drawing the first round of petals, then draw the rest outward in a continuous loopy spiral around and around.

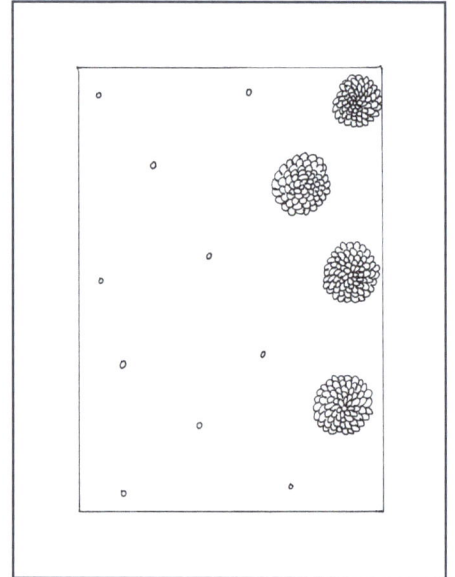

3.   Aw, now go ahead and draw in some little leaf pairs to round out the whole page. Nice!

SWITCH IT UP:

Fill every empty space on the page with flowers. Don't let a bit of page show.

66

PROJECT 30

Triangles 4-ever

Seriously, I love triangles so very much. I hope you do, too, because we are about to draw many of them. This is an easy, meditative page to make, and a great way to end this book.

1.   Start drawing little triangles that connect to each other. You'll find yourself falling into a rhythm of triangle-drawing, so I would definitely listen to music whilst drawing.

2.   You can start at the edge of the page or further in - your call, but fill up the page as far as you want to go. Sometimes it's nice to leave a little white space, and other times you'll want to cover that paper up completely.

SWITCH IT UP:

Draw your triangles in the form of a shape, instead of randomly all over the page. Try a circle, a big triangle, or your first initial.

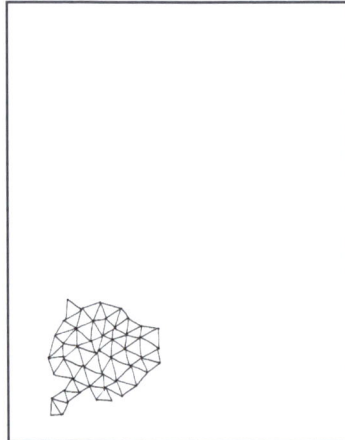

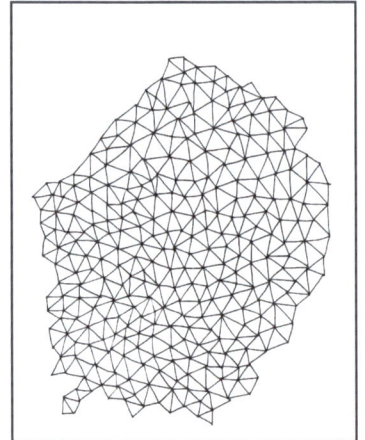

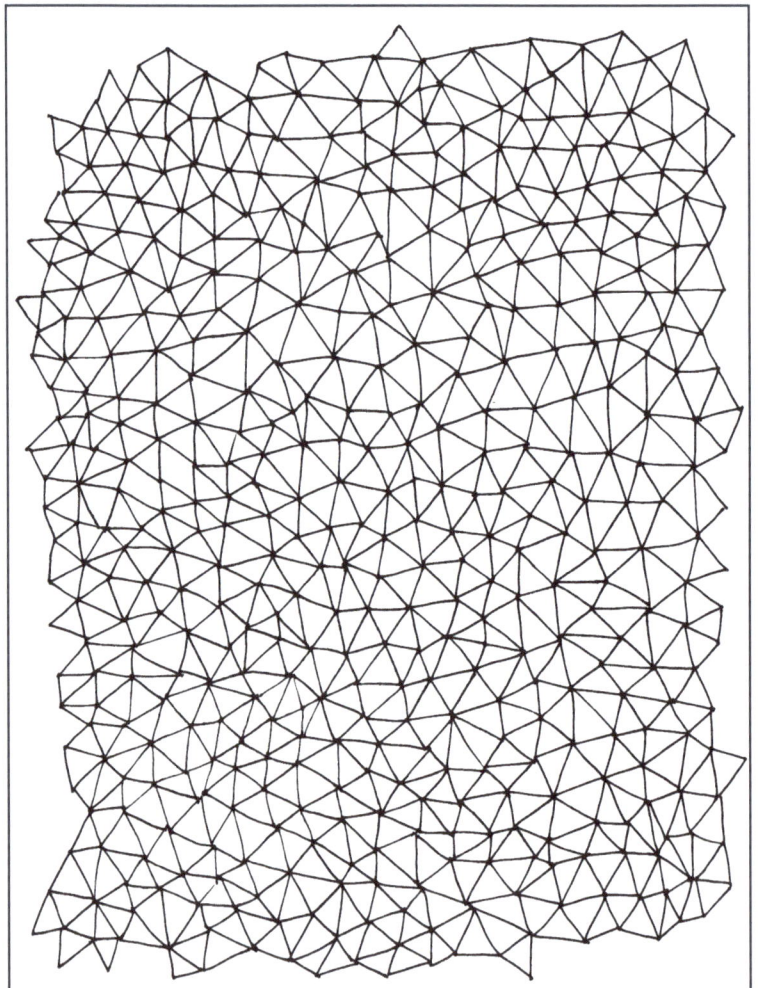

Where to find
pattern ideas

You can find great pattern ideas for adding to your drawings by doing searches on Google or Pinterest.

Try these:

pattern ideas, tangle patterns, tile patterns, Arabic patterns, drawing patterns, doodle ideas.

Alternatively, hole up in your library for a few hours with an expensive beverage, your camera on your phone, and peruse the art and design books for patterns.

Basic Color lesson

Here is a basic color lesson:

Primary colors: Blue, red, yellow.
You can't make primary colors by mixing any other colors together

Secondary colors: Purple, orange, green.

These are pretty straightforward, but then you get into Tertiary colors. Scream it with me:

TERSHEEARRY CULLAAAAAAHS!

These are made by mixing one primary color with one secondary color next to it. Practice on some practice paper if you feel like it.

How to make secondary colors:

◼ Blue + red = purple

◼ Red + yellow = orange

◼ Blue + yellow = green

IDEAS
for coloring

- Try adding texture by making different marks over your base color: dots, hash marks, lines- whatever you like the look of.

- Color in some pages using 2 different types of coloring tools: try a wash of watercolor in some areas, then when that is dry, go back in with colored pencil on top.

- Color some pages using as many colors as you possibly can, and others limiting your palette to 3-4 shades of similar colors.

- Colored pencils and crayons are fun to ombre. Try going from really light to really dark in an area by varying your pressure of the tool on the paper.

- On some pages, use one color in more areas than your other colors, and challenge yourself to limit your colors to 3 or 4 that you like together.

PROJECT 10

PROJECT 1

PROJECT 13

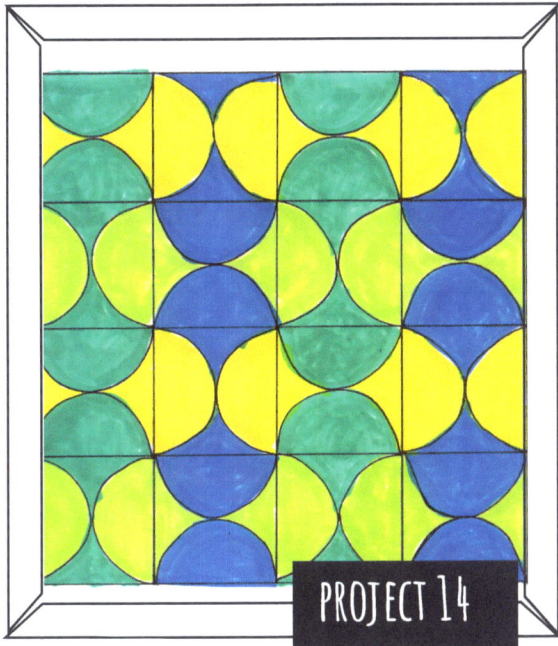

PROJECT 14

PROJECT 26

PROJECT 27

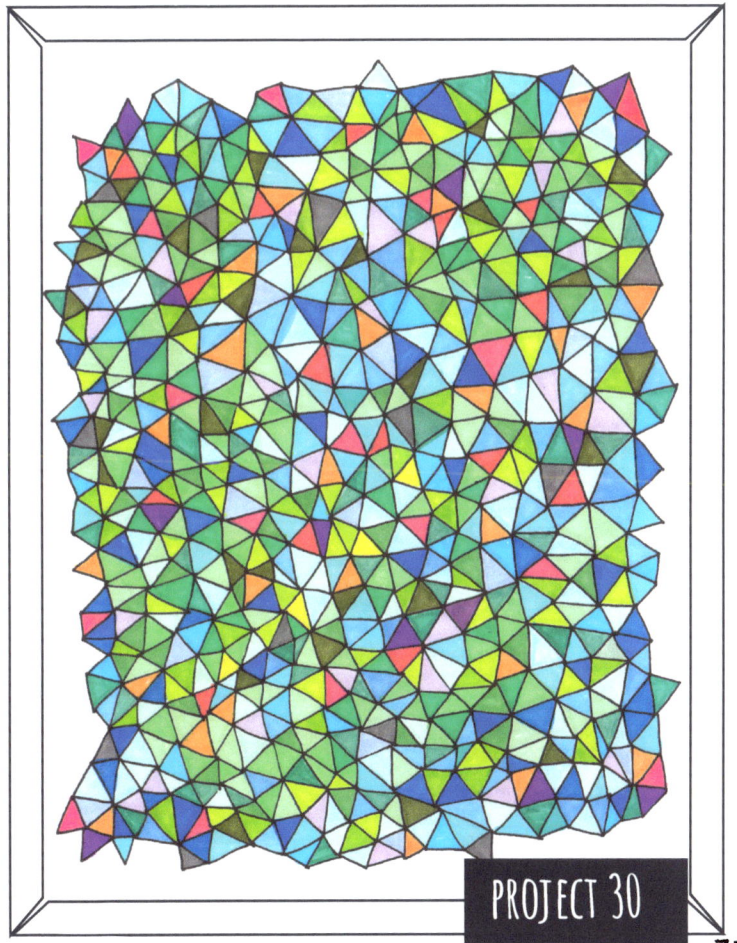

PROJECT 30

Index

www.ingramcontent.com/pod-product-compliance
Lightning Source LLC
Chambersburg PA
CBHW042013080426

42734CB00003B/63